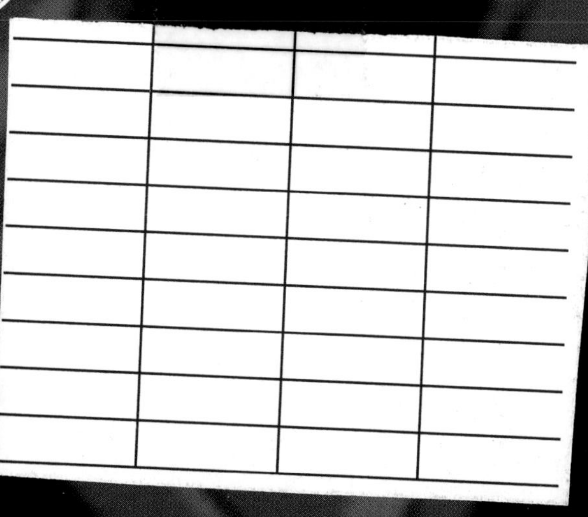

MARVEL
KNIGHTS

story
GREG RUCKA

art
CARLO PAGULAYAN and DANNY MIKI

with JOE BENNETT and GREG HORN

colors
NATHAN EYRING

letters
RS & COMICRAFT's WES & JB

associate managing editor
KELLY LAMY

managing editor
NANCI DAKESIAN

editor
STUART MOORE

editor in chief
JOE QUESADA

president
BILL JEMAS

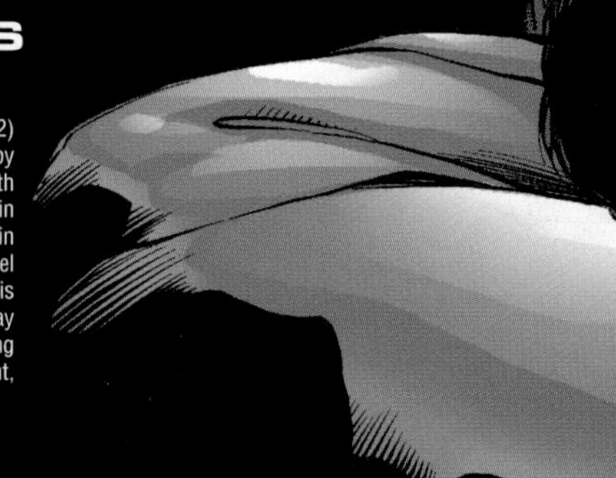

ELEKTRA VOL. 1: INTROSPECT. Contains material originally published in magazine form as ELEKTRA (Vol. 2) #10-15, MARVEL KNIGHTS: DOUBLE-SHOT #3 . First printing 2002. ISBN# 0-7851-0973-0. Published by MARVEL COMICS, a division of MARVEL ENTERTAINMENT GROUP, INC. OFFICE OF PUBLICATION: 10 East 40th Street, New York, NY 10016. $16.99 per copy in the U.S. and $27.25 in Canada (GST #R127032852); Canadian Agreement #40668537. **Printed in Canada.** STAN LEE, Chairman Emeritus. For information regarding advertising in Marvel Comics or on Marvel.com, please contact Russell Brown, Executive Vice President, Consumer Products, Promotions and Media Sales at 212-576-8561 or rbrown@marvel.com

10 9 8 7 6 5 4 3 2 1

•INTROSPECT•

ISSUE #10
Greg Horn

NEW YORK.

GATE 9

PASSPORT, PLEASE.
FLIGHT?
AH, OH... SWISSAIR. FLIGHT ONE EIGHT.

FLIGHT EIGHTEEN, THAT'S FROM *BERN?*

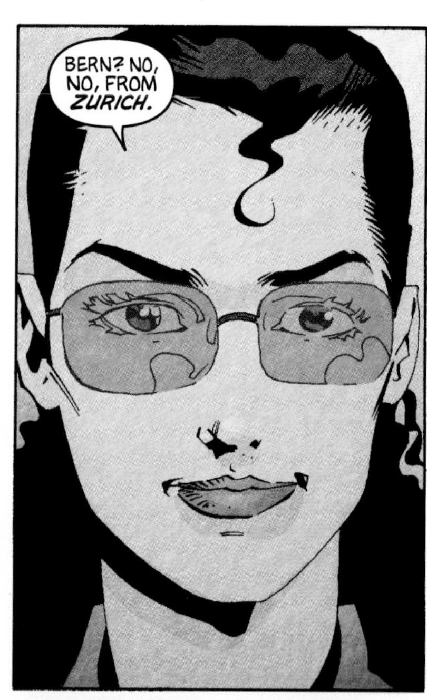
BERN? NO, NO, FROM *ZURICH.*

Destination/Entry date
Destination/Entry date
Destination/Entry date
RIGHT, ZURICH. AND THE *NATURE* OF YOUR VISIT TO *NEW YORK?*

MISS KETTERMAN?
YES?
THE NATURE OF YOUR VISIT, PLEASE?

YES, UHM... HOW TO *SAY,* IS *URLAUB?*
URLAWB?
IT'S *GERMAN,* ALL *RIGHT?* STUPID *BROAD* --

-- DON'T EVEN SPEAK *ENGLISH,* SHE'S SAYING *VACATION,* JESUS --
I WASN'T *ASKING* YOU, SIR.
THIS GONNA TAKE *ALL* DAY?
IF YOU KEEP *INTERRUPTING* ME.

TAKING FOREVER...
HOW LONG ARE YOU PLANNING TO STAY, MISS KETTERMAN?
STAY?
OH, FOR THE LOVE OF --
ONE MORE WORD OUT OF YOU, SIR, AND I'LL HAVE YOU PULLED FROM THE LINE.
STAY. HOW LONG HERE?
OH! TWO WEEKS! TWO WEEKS IN NEW YORK CITY!
SOUNDS LIKE A NICE VACATION.
I... I AM SORRY, I DO NOT UNDERSTAND...
DON'T WORRY ABOUT IT...
...ENJOY YOUR VISIT.

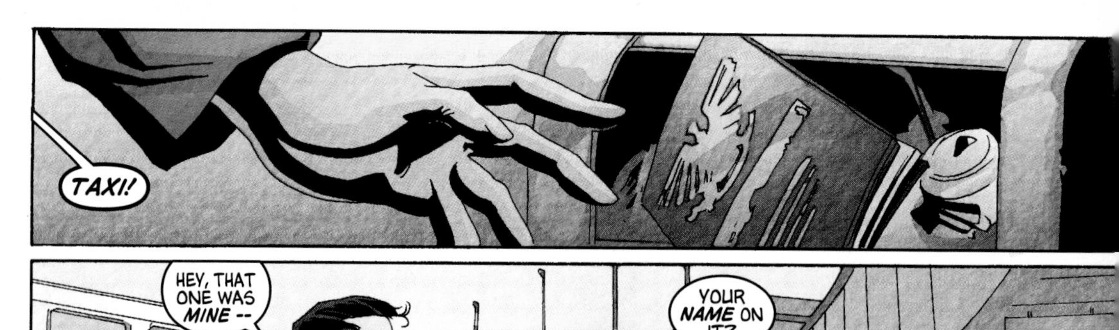
TAXI!

HEY, THAT ONE WAS MINE --
YOUR NAME ON IT?

SIXTY-EIGHTH AND LEX.
KNOW WHERE YOU'RE GOING, HUH?

ALWAYS.

5D

-- NICE TO HAVE YOU **BACK** WITH US, MRS. SALVATORE...
...IT'S BEEN **TOO** LONG.
I WAS IN **MONACO.**

MONACO. I HEAR IT'S **LOVELY** THIS TIME OF --

IT **BORED** ME.

WANT **TICKETS** TO SOMETHING N **BROADWAY** FOR TONIGHT. **TWO TICKETS,** I HAVE A... **FRIEND...** JOINING ME.
OF COURSE, WE'LL **ARRANGE** IT. ANY SHOW IN **PARTICULAR?**
DO I **CARE?** I DO **NOT...**

...AS LONG AS IT DOESN'T **BORE** ME.
NO, WE CAN'T HAVE **THAT,** CAN WE?

TRAMP.

...MESSAGE FOR YOU AT THE DESK.
AND YOU COULDN'T TELL ME THAT WHEN I CHECKED IN?

IT'S ONLY THAT YOU SEEMED IN A HURRY, MRS. SALVATORE --
I WONDER IF I WOULD HAVE THIS PROBLEM AT THE PLAZA?

...WE'D HATE TO THINK YOU WERE UNHAPPY WITH THE SERVICE HERE, MRS. SALVATORE --
PROVE IT TO ME. DO YOU HAVE MY TICKETS?
WE WERE ABLE TO GET TWO TICKETS FOR THE --

GOOD, I'LL ICK THEM P WHEN I ICK UP MY MESSAGE.
YES, VERY GOOD, MRS. SALVATORE--
YOU CAN HANG UP, NOW.

YES, VERY GOOD, MRS. --
CHK

1 9

MRS. SALVATORE
32
HERE.
THEY'RE FOR TONIGHT.
USE THEM, SCALP THEM, WHATEVER.

EL LOCO
¡HOLA, NICOLE!
⟨CECE! HOW'S THE FAMILY?⟩
⟨DON'T ASK! CESAR GOT ARRESTED AGAIN, AND PAPA'S DIABETES IS JUST WORSE AND WORSE.⟩
⟨LOOKING FOR DANNY?⟩
⟨HE HERE?⟩
⟨SAME BOOTH AS EVER, NICOLE...⟩
⟨...SOME THINGS NEVER CHANGE!⟩
⟨TELL ME ABOUT IT!⟩
⟨LATER!⟩

‹BEEN A WHILE.›
‹JUST **STORAGE?!**›
‹YES. SOMEPLACE SAFE. SAME **PRICE?!**›
‹YOU KNOW IT.›

‹YOU'RE DRAWING **ATTENTION.**›

‹I DON'T KNOW **WHAT** YOU'RE TALKING ABOUT.›

‹SEE YOU AROUND.›

LOCA.

‹LET'S DO IT.›
‹COME ON. I HAVE SOMEWHERE TO BE.›
‹LET'S DO IT.›
‹FINE. I'LL GO FIRST.›

<G-GU-GUH YOU YOU'RE CRAZY YOU -->

‹YOU STARTED IT.›

WHAT?
THIRTY-TWO.
WHERE IS SHE?
UP TOP. SHE'S EXPECTING YOU.

WEAPON.
YOU ARE LATE.
WHAT DO YOU HAVE FOR ME?
NOTHING.

THEN WHY DID YOU CONTACT ME?
YOU ARE DRAWING ATTENTION, WEAPON.
S.H.I.E.L.D.
INTERPOL.
I COME TO YOU FOR WORK, NOT LECTURES, DEE.
THEN YOU COME IN VAIN, WEAPON.
I HAVE NO WORK FOR YOU.
BUT THERE IS WORK TO BE DONE?
THERE IS ALWAYS SOMEONE WHO NEEDS TO DIE, WEAPON...
...JUST AS THERE IS ALWAYS SOMEONE WILLING TO PAY TO MAKE IT HAPPEN.
YET YOU OFFER ME NOTHING.
WHY DID YOU WANT TO MEET?

BECAUSE I AM FOND OF YOU, WEAPON.
BECAUSE I WANT THE BEST FOR YOU.
THEN LET ME WORK.
IT IS BECOMING TOO DANGEROUS.
TOO MUCH ATTENTION IS ON YOU.
THAT IS MY CHOICE. MY RISK.
YOU KNOW BETTER. IT IS ALL OUR RISK.
THOSE WHO HIRE YOU. THOSE WHO MEDIATE FOR YOU. THOSE WHO BANK FOR YOU.
THOSE WHO MAKE YOUR PAPERS. WHO SELL YOU YOUR WEAPONS. WHO BUILD YOUR TOOLS.
A THOUSAND PEOPLE AROUND THE WORLD, SURVIVING IN ANONYMITY TO SERVE WEAPONS LIKE YOU.
AND WHEN YOU ARE WEAK, YOU THREATEN US ALL.
DEE. DO NOT THREATEN ME.
THEN DO NOT THREATEN US.

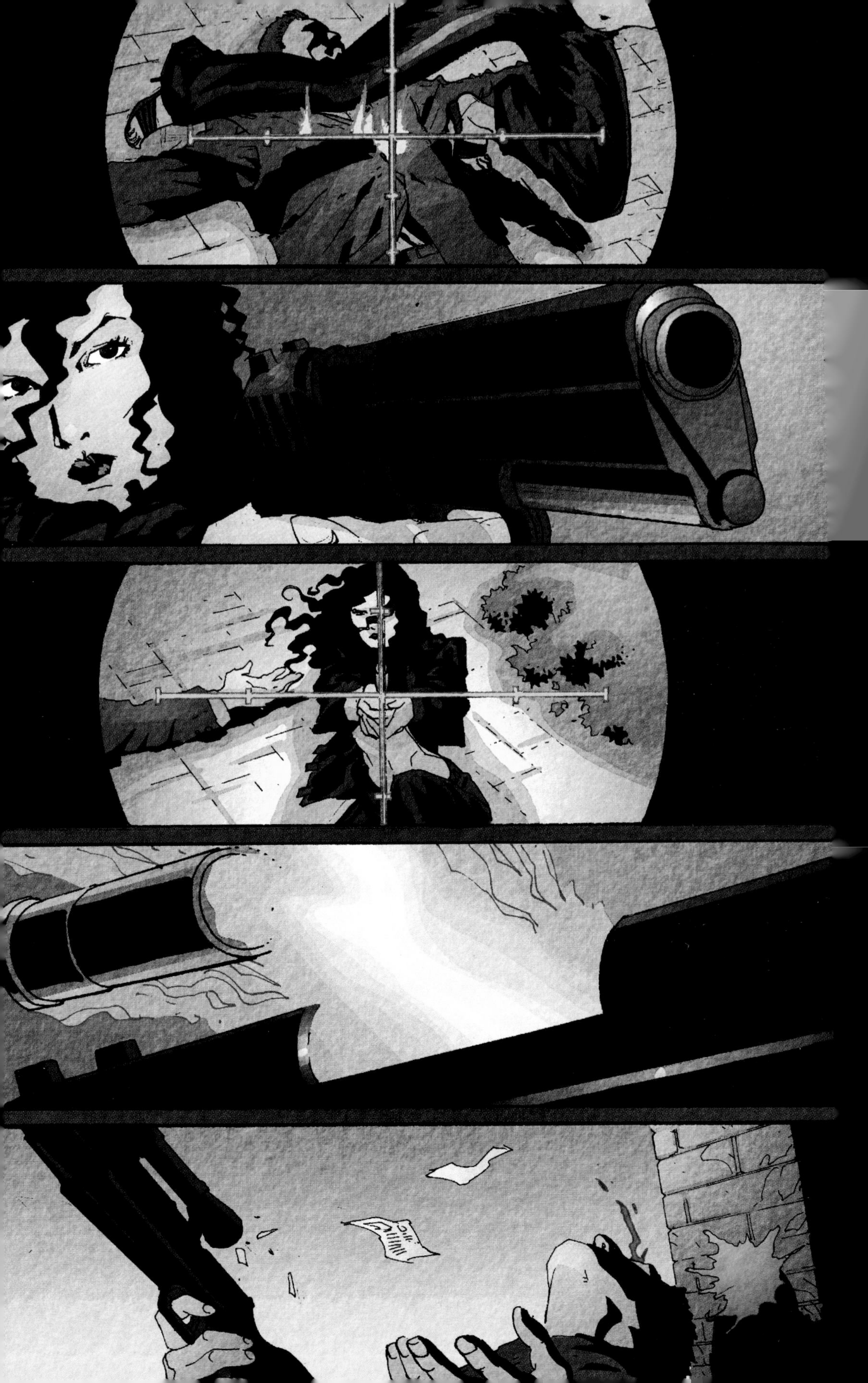

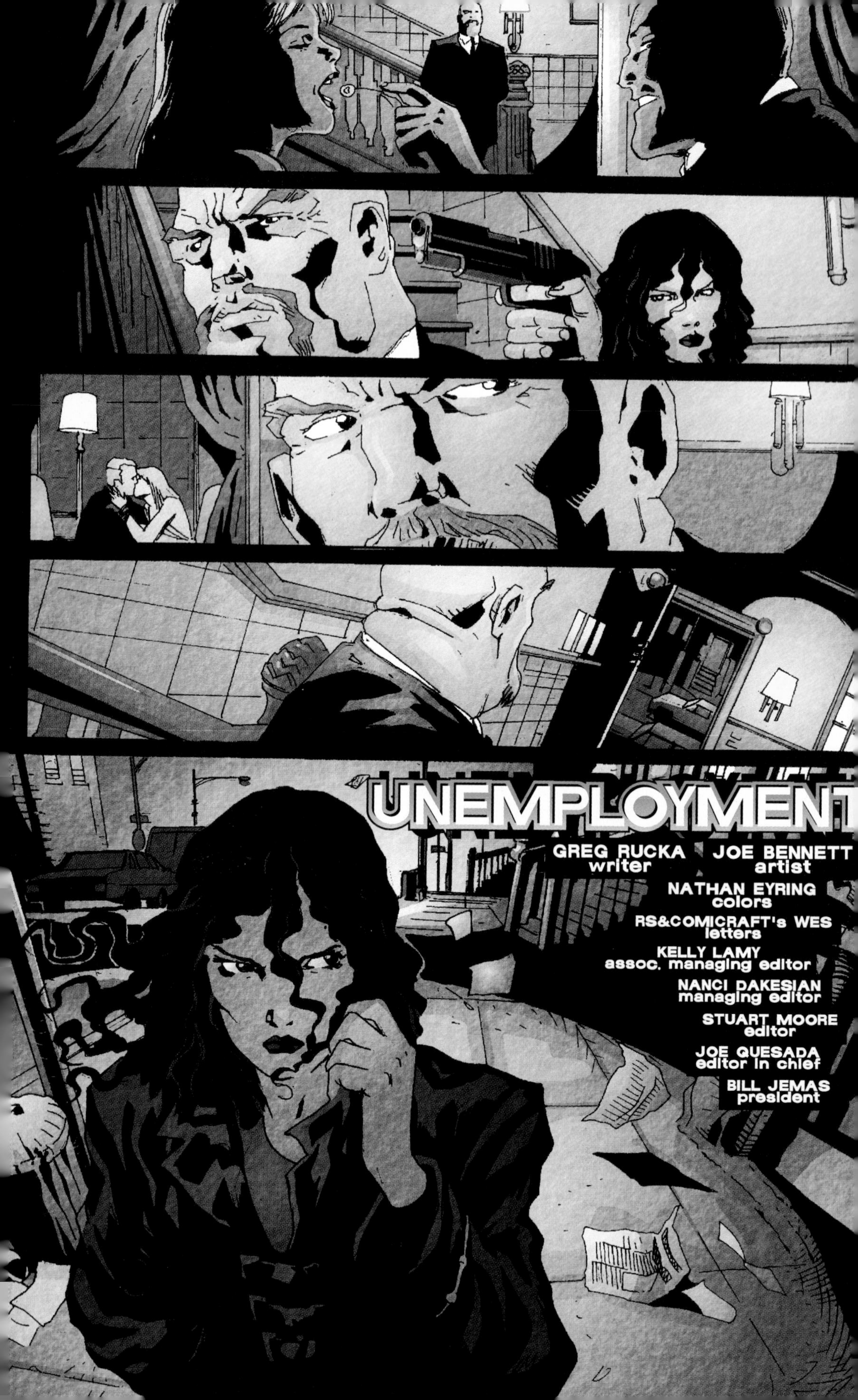

UNEMPLOYMENT
GREG RUCKA writer
JOE BENNETT artist
NATHAN EYRING colors
RS&COMICRAFT's WES letters
KELLY LAMY assoc. managing editor
NANCI DAKESIAN managing editor
STUART MOORE editor
JOE QUESADA editor in chief
BILL JEMAS president

ISSUE #11
Greg Horn

Los Angeles.
Tonight.
‹...bring that over here...›
‹-- another one, but hot this time --›
‹-- to my sister, you touch her again --›

‹-- AND I'LL SPLIT YOU OPEN...›
‹WHAT'S THAT SMELL...?›
‹LOOKS LIKE SOMEONE GOT LOST, HUH?›
HEY, JUNKIE...
...YOU JUST WANDERED INTO THE WRONG PARTY.
YOU LEAVE BEFORE YOU GET HU--
HKKKK... HUKKKK...

PAUL
LIVE
CRIME LAB
MORE.
GREG RUCKA writer
CARLO PAGULAYAN penciler
DANNY MIKI inker
NATHAN EYRING colors
RS&COMICRAFT's WES letters
KELLY LAMY assoc. managing editor
NANCI DAKESIAN managing editor
STUART MOORE editor
JOE QUESADA editor in chief
BILL JEMAS president

NEW YORK.
ONE MONTH AGO.
...AND THE NEW ISSUE OF LE MONDE.
YOUR CHANGE.
SO, WHAT? YOU DOING RESEARCH?
SORRY?
MOST FOLKS BUY THEIR PAPERS ONE AT A TIME IS ALL.
YOU LOOKING FOR SOMETHING IN PARTICULAR? OR YOU JUST ONE OF THOSE NUTS WHO'S LIKE AN INFORMATION JUNKIE?
I NEED A JOB.
I HEAR THEY'RE HIRING AT THE POST OFFICE.
NEWS

T-T-T-T-T TRAVEL OPPORTUNITIES
WANTED: Guide for White Water trp, inquire 831.555.8824. Prv. Exp a must.
RENTAL: Cote d'Azure, on the Med, btfl view, 6 wk aval Aug. Call: 01 44 121
SUPERBOWL!
FORENSICS AND CRIME LAB ON SUPERBOWL SECURITY
DAMMIT.

MIAMI.
THREE WEEKS AGO.

Graphic MEDIA
SITE
...GET THE TICKETS TO SEE THESE GUYS...
-- NO, NO, TWO HUNDRED SHARES --
...SAID SHE WASN'T SEEING OTHER PEOPLE...

...SOLD OUT WITHIN HOURS IF YOU CAN BELIEVE THAT...
-- THEN SELL IT FOR GOD'S SAKE, I MEAN, REALLY --
...THEN WHO DO I SEE HER WITH? CLAUDIA, OF COURSE, I MEAN...

No New Messag
0 of 0 Unread
Index
...IT'S LIKE SHE JUST DOESN'T FEEL ANYTHING...

No New Messages
0 of 0 Unread
Index
Archive
...DUNNO, MAYBE ONE-FIFTY A HEAD?...

...THINK
IT'S ABOUT THE MONEY IT'S NEVER --
...EATS ME UP INSIDE...
No New Messages
...WELL, LIKE A NEED I GUESS, I DON'T KNOW...
...SUPPOSED TO LIVE ANYWAY...
...JUST DOESN'T STOP HURTING...
...JUST DOESN'T EVER STOP...
...DRIVING ME CRAZY --
CONNECTED COFFEE

RIO DE JANEIRO.
TWO WEEKS AGO.

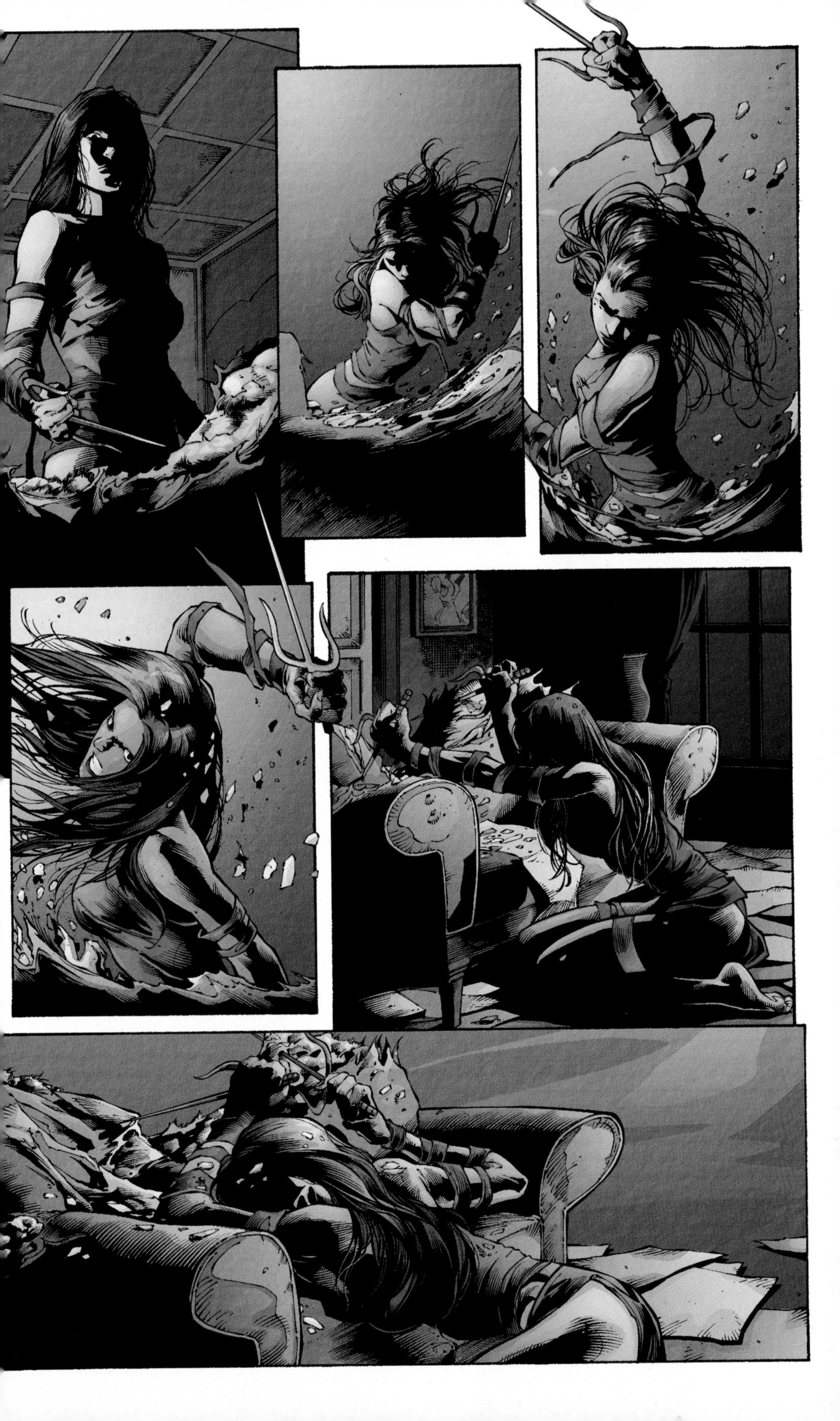

...PLEASE...
...GIVE ME WORK...

DA DEEP

1 New Message
1 of 1 Unread
CLK KLK
XXX HOT HOT HOT XXX
THE YOUNGEST, FRESHEST, HOTTEST GIRLS ON THE PLANET!!
Click HERE for FREE TRIAL!

PARIS.
TWELVE DAYS AGO.
‹...SAY YOUR NAME WAS?›
‹TELL HIM IT'S GISELLE.›

‹JUST A MOMENT.›

JOHN LAWRENCE PHEONIX UPLINK
MENU

JAGER
‹GISELLE?›
‹YOU MUST BE CLAUDE.›
‹WHY DON'T YOU COME IN?›
MAN
‹WE WERE NEVER TO MEET, GISELLE.›
‹THE LAST SHIPMENT WAS PREPARED EXACTLY TO YOUR SPECIFICATIONS, RIGHT TO METHOD OF DELIVERY.›
‹IF THERE WAS A PROBLEM, YOU SHOULD HAVE CONTACTED ME IN THE USUAL FASHION --›
‹YOUR WORK HAS BEEN EXCEPTIONAL, CLAUDE...›
‹...DON'T FEAR ME.›
‹I MEAN YOU NO HARM.›
‹A RELIEF, TO BE SURE.›

‹BUT A SHORT-LIVED ONE.›
‹WE WERE NEVER TO MEET IN PERSON.›
‹I WAS NOT FOLLOWED. I HAVE TOLD NO ONE OF YOU, OR WHAT YOU DO FOR ME.›

‹SMALL COMFORT, MY DEAR GISELLE. I AM MORE CONCERNED WITH HOW YOU LOCATED ME IN THE FIRST PLACE.›
‹OUR CONTACT HAS ALWAYS BEEN ANONYMOUS.›

‹I KNOW EVERYONE WHO DOES WORK FOR ME.›
‹THE AMOUNT I PAY FOR YOUR SERVICES, I WOULD BE A FOOL NOT TO.›

‹VERY WELL. I SUPPOSE, THEN, YOU WISH TO TALK BUSINESS?›
‹I HAVE A CONTACT AT NATO WHO CAN PROVIDE ME WITH THE LATEST PROTOTYPES IN SONIC TECHNOLOGY...›
‹...IF YOU'RE INTERESTED --›
‹I AM NOT.›
‹I DON'T NEED TECH, CLAUDE...›

‹...I NEED WORK.›

‹...I BEG YOUR PARDON?›
‹WORK. A JOB.›

‹THERE'S NOTHING OUT THERE.›
‹I'VE HAD NO WORK... FOR MONTHS, NOW.›

‹YOU HAVE MY SYMPATHY, GISELLE.›
‹BUT I HAVE NEVER BEEN A CONTRACTOR. CERTAINLY NOT IN THE KIND OF WORK YOU DESIRE.›

‹I'M AFRAID I CANNOT HELP YOU.›
‹...I SEE.›

‹THANK YOU FOR YOUR TIME, CLAUDE.›
‹DON'T WORRY...›

‹...YOU'LL NEVER SEE ME AGAIN.›

PRAGUE, NINE DAYS AGO.
‹...BELIEVE YOU WOULD COME HERE LOOKING!›
‹I HAVE NOTHING FOR YOU. NOW --›

ST. PETERSBURG, EIGHT DAYS AGO.
‹-- GO! IF WE ARE EVEN SEEN TOGETHER, IT WOULD BE FATAL FOR BOTH OF US!›

KYOTO, SEVEN DAYS AGO.
‹...TELL YOU EVEN IF I DID HAVE SOMETHING, I SURE AS HELL WOULDN'T HAND IT TO YOU RIGHT NOW...›

SYDNEY, SIX DAYS AGO.
...SEEN YOURSELF? YOU'RE FALLING APART...

SEATTLE, FIVE DAYS AGO.
...WOULDN'T TRUST YOU WITH THAT KIND OF WORK EVEN IF I HAD IT TO BEGIN WITH.
YOU WANT SOME ADVICE, NICOLE? EITHER GO BACK ON WHATEVER IT WAS YOU WERE TAKING...

...OR GET SOME PROFESSIONAL HELP.

GENEVIÈVE
RESTAURANT
SELF-DEFENSE
FOKMA
COMBAT AIKIDO JUDO
KARATE KENDO
NOW ACCEPTING
STUDENTS
know
feel
think
2nd Annual
Tournament
YOU LOOK *LOST.*
...I *AM*...
...PLEASE...
He w
...WILL YOU *FIGHT* ME?

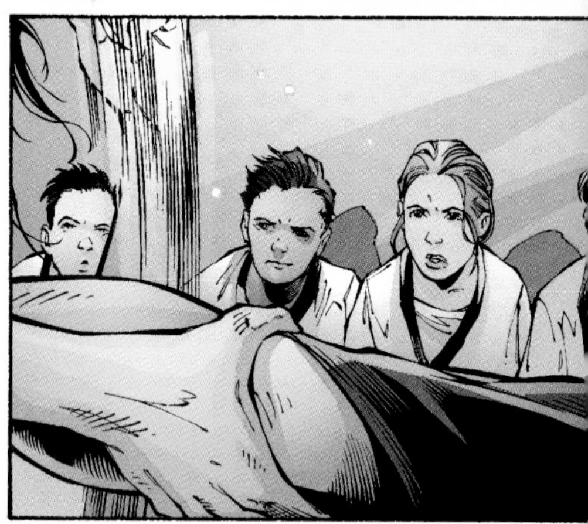

GUHAAAAHUH
KRRRK
MORE.
HUHUHUHUH
PLEASE.
HUHUHUHUUUU

ACCEPTING
STUDENTS

FOKMA

CLASS
HOURS
5 PM-8PM

CLASS
HOURS
5 PM-8PM
MISTER LOCKE?
I THINK I **FOUND** HER...

LOS ANGELES.
NOW.

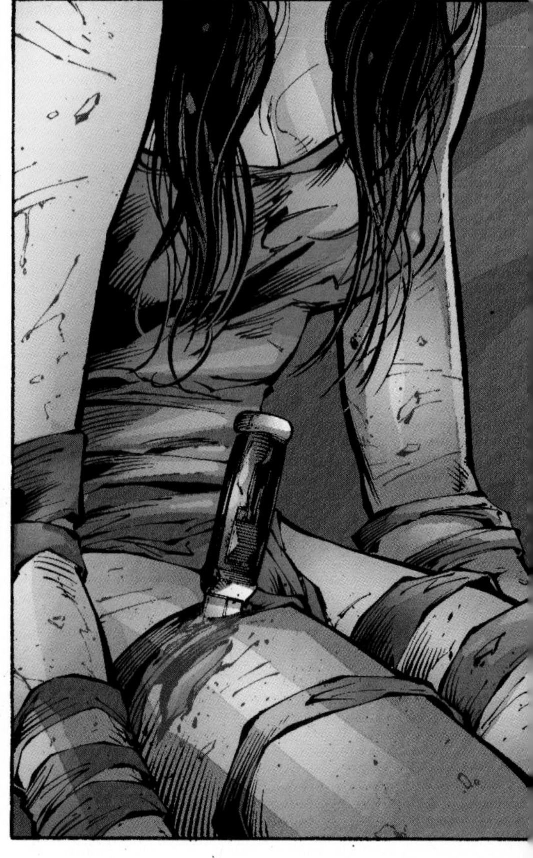

NO, NO, NO.
YOU DON'T GET TO DIE YET.
I KNOW, I KNOW, I SOUND LIKE A LUNATIC OR SOMETHING.
IT'S THE JOY, I SUPPOSE.
I JUST CAN'T TELL YOU HOW HAPPY I AM TO SEE YOU...

...WELL, TO SEE YOU LIKE THIS, AT LEAST.
TO THINK, IT ONLY TOOK A MONTH. WELL...
...A MONTH AND THEN FOUR YEARS, TOO.
MY NAME IS JEREMY LOCKE.
MEANS NOTHING TO YOU, I'M SURE.
IT TOOK ME A LONG TIME JUST TO LEARN YOUR NAME.
ELEKTRA NATCHIOS.
KNOWING THAT WAS IMPORTANT TO ME...
...BECAUSE I'M GOING TO DESTROY YOU.

ISSUE #12

SOUTH CENTRAL LOS ANGELES.
WHAT DID YOU GIVE HER?
PRIMO'S
SCOPOLAMINE WITH MORPHINE. IT'S THE SAME STUFF THE C.I.A. USES WHEN THEY WANT TO SOFT TRANSFER PEOPLE...
...WON'T PUT HER OUT COMPLETELY, BUT IT'S ENOUGH TO DROP HER INTO A TWILIGHT STATE.
SHE CAN HEAR US, BUT IT'S LIKE SHE'S DREAMING.
WILL SHE REMEMBER WHAT SHE HEARS?
IF SHE FOCUSES, YES.
...WH... WHERE...
HUSH...
...YOU'LL GET THE WHERE AND THE WHY SOON ENOUGH, ELEKTRA NATCHIOS...
...ALL IN GOOD TIME.

HOLLYWOOD
THANK YOU, PHILIP...
...I'LL BE IN MY OFFICE.
LET ME KNOW WHEN WE'RE *READY.*
YES, SIR, MISTER LOCKE.

HARVARD UNIVERSITY
Jeremy K. Locke
THE TRUSTEES OF COLUMBIA UNIVERSITY IN THE CITY OF NEW YORK
OCTORATE OF JURISPRUDENCE
JEREMY KYLE LOCKE
tanford University
eremy K. Locke

SHE'S *HERE,* BREE.

I FINALLY GOT HER.
MISTER LOCKE?
WE'RE ALL READY FOR YOU.

WONDERFUL.

INTROSPECT

TIME

SORRY TO KEEP YOU *WAITING...*

...AND MY APOLOGIES FOR THE RESTRAINTS, AS WELL.
THEY'RE DEGRADING, I REALIZE THAT, BUT I'M SURE YOU UNDERSTAND WHY THEY'RE NECESSARY.
YOU'RE A VERY DANGEROUS WOMAN, AND I CAN'T TAKE ANY CHANCES...
...ESPECIALLY AFTER WAITING SO LONG FOR THIS OPPORTUNITY.
YOU'RE ROLLY.
YES... I SUPPOSE I AM.
AND YOU'RE DOPEY...
...AND WHAT SHOULD WE CALL HIM?
BIG.
ALL RIGHT, WE'LL CALL HIM BIG.
'BIG,' IF YOU'LL PUT THESE UP ON THE SCREEN WHEN I ASK FOR THEM. THEY'RE ALREADY IN ORDER.
YES, SIR.

ELEKTRA?

ELEKTRA. I REALLY NEED YOU TO PAY ATTENTION, NOW.
YES, THAT'S RIGHT.
FOR THIS TO WORK YOU HAVE TO FOCUS, OKAY?
CAN YOU DO THAT FOR ME? CAN YOU FOCUS?
NO. NO. ELEKTRA, LISTEN.
I NEED YOU TO FOCUS.
FO-CUS?
THAT'S RIGHT, CAN YOU DO THAT?
UH-HUH.
GOOD.

I WANT YOU TO FOCUS BECAUSE I WANT YOU TO UNDERSTAND WHAT YOU ARE.
AND HOW MUCH YOU SHOULD HATE YOURSELF.

THAT'S...
...ME...?
THAT'S RIGHT...
...THAT'S YOU.
...PAPA...?
THAT'S RIGHT, THAT'S YOU WITH YOUR PAPA --
-- NEXT PLEASE, MISTER CARSON --
-- AND THERE YOU ARE AGAIN.
DO YOU REMEMBER HOW OLD YOU WERE THEN, ELEKTRA?
...TWELVE...
THAT'S CORRECT, YOU'D JUST TURNED TWELVE -- NEXT ONE, PLEASE --
-- AND HERE YOU ARE AT FIFTEEN, IN ROME, I THINK.
YOU WERE VERY GOOD, YOU KNOW THAT? YOU WERE OLYMPIC CALIBER.
...PAPA...
YES, WE'RE GETTING TO THAT.
NEXT.

THERE HE IS AGAIN.
NEXT.
...NNOOO...
BRINGS BACK BAD MEMORIES, DOES IT? IT WOULD FOR ME, TOO...
...NOOO NO NO GO AWAY...
IT'LL BE GONE IN A MOMENT, ELEKTRA.
I NEED YOU TO KNOW THAT I UNDERSTAND HOW HE DIED, IF NOT WHY.
IT'S AWFUL, ISN'T IT?
IT HURTS.
NEXT.

THIS ONE'S *IMPORTANT,* ELEKTRA.
THIS IS THE *CRUX* OF THE WHOLE *PROBLEM,* RIGHT HERE...
NO... NO NO NONO --
-- NOLOOKING WON'TLOOKING --
-- DON'TWANTTO --
LOOK AT IT.
LOOK AT IT.
LOOK AT IT!

THAT'S RIGHT. THAT'S IT.
THAT'S YOU.
THAT'S YOU DYING.
THAT'S YOU DEAD.
...STOP...
YOU WERE DEAD.
...PLEASE STOP...

YOU WERE DEAD...
...YOU SHOULD BE DEAD.
YEAH.
YOU KNOW IT'S TRUE.

NEXT ONE, PLEASE.
THIS ONE IS BETTER. I THINK YOU'LL LIKE THIS ONE.

...OH!

THOUGHT YOU'D LIKE THIS ONE.
YOU WOULDN'T BELIEVE WHAT WENT THROUG TO GET IT, EITHER.
THIS WAS TAKEN ABOUT TWO YEARS AGO, IN SAINT PETERSBURG.
IT'S REALLY SOMETHING, ISN'T IT?
UH-HUH.
ALL THOSE MEN WITH GUNS, AND THERE YOU ARE, JUST YOUR SKILL AND YOUR SAI, AND THEY'RE NO MATCH FOR YOU.
YOU'RE PROUD OF THAT, AREN'T YOU?
UH-HUH.
DO YOU KNOW WHAT YOU WERE DOING THERE?
UH-HUH.
CAN YOU TELL ME WHAT YO WERE DOING THERE ELEKTRA?

FIGHTING.
NO.
YOU THINK THAT'S WHAT YOU WERE DOING, BUT THAT'S NOT WHAT YOU WERE DOING.
NEXT.
YOU WEREN'T FIGHTING, ELEKTRA...
..YOU WERE KILLING.
YOU KILLED SEVEN MEN THAT DAY, NOT COUNTING THE ONE YOU WERE AFTER.
SEVEN.
NEXT.

HERE'S ANOTHER FIVE.
NEXT.
AND ANOTHER SIX.
NEXT.
FIVE MORE. ONE OF THEM'S IN THE BEDROOM.
NEXT.
THREE MORE.
NEXT.
AND ANOTHER THREE. HOW OLD DO YOU THINK THE BOY WAS?
NEXT.
OH, YES, THIS ONE... ELEVEN AT ONCE, I SUPPOSE SOME PEOPLE WOULD CALL THAT IMPRESSIVE.
NEXT.
ONLY TWO, HERE. BOTH COPS I UNDERSTAND.
NEXT.
NO...

...MORE!
NO MORE!
NO MORENO MORE --
CARSON!
NO MORE!
CARSON, GET DOWN HERE!
HURRY!
SHE'S TRYING TO GET...
...FREE...

OH GOD.
TELL ME --
-- WHY ≥HUFF≤

-- NO --
-- MORE --
-- DRUGS!
ANSWER ME!

GHUHH
WHO ARE YOU?
WHAT DO YOU WANT?
CHKSS
WHY ARE YOU -- ARE --
-- YOU... DOING...
...THIS...

NO DISRESPECT, MISTER LOCKE, BUT I HAVE TO ASK YOU.
WOULDN'T IT JUST BE EASIER IF YOU LET ME HANDLE THIS?
YOU MEAN PUT A BULLET IN HER HEAD AND THEN DUMP HER IN THE PACIFIC?

I'M NOT... EAGER TO DO IT. BUT IT'S NOT LIKE ANYONE WOULD MISS HER.
AND IT WOULD BE A HELL OF A LOT SAFER.
IT WOULD.

BUT THEN WE'D BECOME HER.

I'LL BE IN MY OFFICE.
LET ME KNOW WHEN WE'RE READY TO RESUME.

--ELEKTRA, WAKE UP.
GOOD.
I'M GOING TO ASK YOU NOT TO DO THAT AGAIN, OKAY? WE'RE ALMOST FINISHED HERE, AND AS SOON AS WE'RE DONE, YOU'LL BE FREE TO GO.
YOU ASKED WHY.
IT'S A FAIR QUESTION, THOUGH NOT AS IMPORTANT TO YOU AS WHAT.
SPECIFICALLY, WHAT AM I PLANNING ON DOING WITH YOU.
TURN IT ON.
HER NAME WAS SABRINA COLE.
SHE WAS A FEDERAL PROSECUTOR.
YOU MURDERED HER, AND THE THING OF IT IS, ELEKTRA...
...SHE WASN'T EVEN YOUR TARGET.
NEXT.

THIS MAN *WAS.* TERRENCE BARBUR. HE DEALT AND SMUGGLED *DRUGS,* LOTS OF THEM, MOSTLY FROM SOUTHEAST ASIA.
AND HE GOT *ARRESTED,* AS CRIMINALS SOMETIMES GET ARRESTED, AND THE PEOPLE HE DID BUSINESS WITH BECAME *AFRAID.*

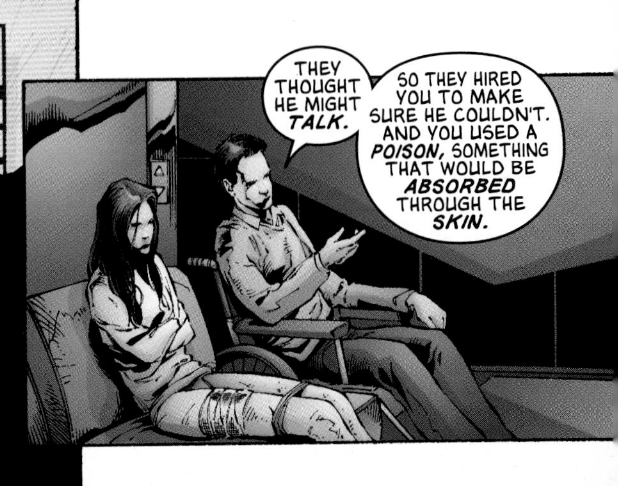
THEY THOUGHT HE MIGHT *TALK.*
SO THEY HIRED YOU TO MAKE SURE HE COULDN'T. AND YOU USED A *POISON,* SOMETHING THAT WOULD BE *ABSORBED* THROUGH THE *SKIN.*

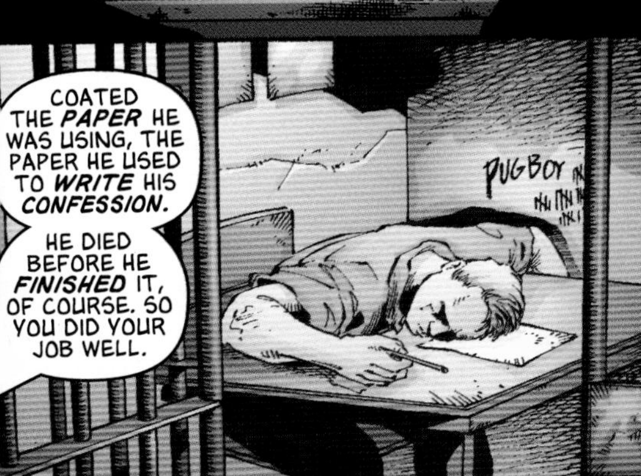
COATED THE *PAPER* HE WAS USING, THE PAPER HE USED TO *WRITE* HIS *CONFESSION.*
HE DIED BEFORE HE *FINISHED* IT, OF COURSE. SO YOU DID YOUR JOB WELL.
PUGBOY

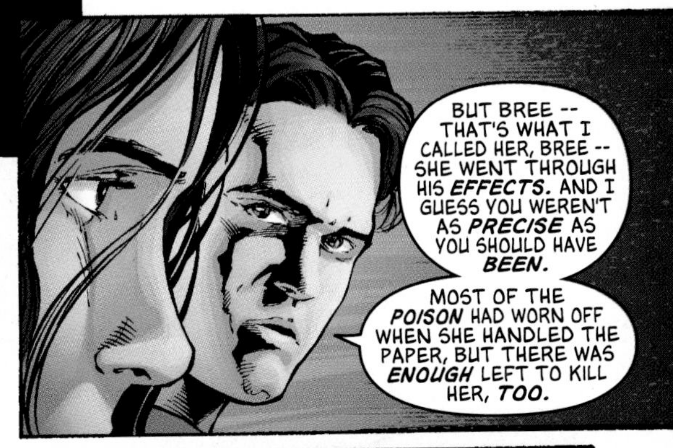
BUT BREE -- THAT'S WHAT I CALLED HER, BREE -- SHE WENT THROUGH HIS *EFFECTS.* AND I GUESS YOU WEREN'T AS *PRECISE* AS YOU SHOULD HAVE *BEEN.*
MOST OF THE *POISON* HAD WORN OFF WHEN SHE HANDLED THE PAPER, BUT THERE WAS *ENOUGH* LEFT TO KILL HER, *TOO.*

IT TOOK A LOT *LONGER,* THOUGH.
IT TOOK SEVENTEEN *DAYS.*
SHE DIED THE DAY BEFORE OUR *WEDDING.*
SO, THAT'S THE *WHY.*
NOW I'M GOING TO EXPLAIN THE *WHAT.*

"MISTER CARSON IS GOING TO GIVE YOU ANOTHER SHOT OF THAT DOSE HE'S PREPARED, A BIG ONE. IT'LL PUT YOU OUT UNTIL TOMORROW NIGHT.
"THEN HE'S GOING TO TAKE YOU OUT TO THE MOJAVE. AND THEN HE'S GOING TO LET YOU GO, ELEKTRA.
"I'M NOT LIKE YOU, ELEKTRA. I DON'T BELIEVE IN MURDER. NOT EVEN IN THE GUISE OF SEEKING JUSTICE.
"BUT I TRULY DON'T THINK YOU DESERVE THE LIFE YOU HAVE.
"YOU'RE A KILLER. THAT'S ALL YOU ARE. I THINK THAT'S ALL YOU CAN BE. YOU'VE BEEN BLESSED WITH TWO LIVES, AND STILL, ALL YOU CAN DO IS MURDER.
"YOU'RE ADDICTED TO IT, TO VIOLENCE AND TO KILLING. YOU GIVE NOTHING. YOU SERVE NOTHING. YOU JUST TAKE.
"YOU TAKE LIFE.
"BUT NOT ANYMORE. I'VE PUT YOU OUT OF BUSINESS. IT TOOK ME YEARS TO MAKE IT HAPPEN, BUT YOU'VE ALREADY SEEN THE RESULT. NO ONE WILL HIRE YOU.
"SO YOU'LL BE FREE. BUT YOU WON'T BE ABLE TO DO THE ONE THING THAT GIVES YOUR LIFE MEANING.
"AND I DON'T THINK YOU'LL BE ABLE TO HANDLE IT. I THINK YOU'LL END UP KILLING YOURSELF, EITHER BY YOUR OWN HAND, OR BY FORCING THE HAND OF ANOTHER.
"BECAUSE WHEN YOU REALLY LOOK AT YOURSELF, ELEKTRA, YOU'LL HAVE TO CONFRONT THE TRUTH.
"THAT YOU'RE A MONSTER...
"...AND YOU DON'T DESERVE TO LIVE."

ISSUE #13
Greg Horn

INTROSPECT
PART THREE

HOLLYWOOD HILLS.
-- BEHIND OUR BACKS, LOCKE!
-- WAS AN AGREEMENT IN PLACE --
-- DON'T CARE ABOUT THAT, I WANT TO KNOW WHERE THAT WHORE IS NOW!
I LET HER GO.
OH, FOR THE LOVE --
YOU HAD BETTER BE JOKING, BOY!
WELL, LET'S FIND OUT, COLONEL FISCHER.
MISTER CARSON, DID ELEKTRA GET OFF ALL RIGHT?

THE FINAL DOSE WAS WEARING OFF ABOUT THE TIME I LET HER GO, MISTER LOCKE.
YOU GAVE HER THE KEYS? AND HER GEAR?
AS YOU REQUESTED, YES SIR.
LAST I SAW OF HER, SHE WAS WANDERING DOWN THE ROAD.
AND HOW'D SHE LOOK?
DIFFICULT TO SAY. SHE DIDN'T SPEAK ONCE. BARELY EVEN REACTED WHEN I DROPPED THE KEYS IN FRONT OF HER.
I THINK YOU HIT HER WHERE SHE LIVES.
THERE YOU GO.
NO, THERE WE DO NOT GO, LOCKE!
DAMMIT, MAN! THE TIME, THE MONEY, THE WORK WE PUT INTO THIS, YOU WEREN'T SUPPOSED TO RELEASE HER!
YOU WERE SUPPOSED TO KILL HER!

CHK
CHK
CHK
CHK

CHK
CHK
CHK
CHK
CHK
CHK
CHK
CHK
CHK
CHK
CHK
CHK
CHK
CHK
CHK
SSSSSSs
SSSs

...DO YOU HEAR WHAT YOU'RE SAYING? ASIDE FROM THE GROSS MORALIZING, YOU OVERSTEPPED YOUR BOUNDS!
WE FORMED THIS... COALITION... FOR ONE PURPOSE, LOCKE, AND ONE PURPOSE ALONE.

REVENGE.
REVENGE FOR WHAT THAT ASSASSIN DID TO EACH OF US.

I THINK THAT'S EXACTLY WHAT I'VE GOTTEN, MISTER KURTIS.
PLEASE! YOU LET HER GO, YOU RETURN TO HER HER FREEDOM, AND YOU CALL THAT REVENGE?

HER BEATING HEART IN MY HAND, THAT WOULD BE REVENGE!
HER PLEAS FOR MY MERCY, THAT WOULD BE REVENGE!

BUT NOT YOUR SQUEAMISH EXCUSE FOR JUSTICE.
THAT IS LESS THAN NOTHING. THAT IS WORTHLESS.

TO YOU, PERHAPS. BUT I SAID AT THE START THAT I WOULD NOT BECOME WHAT I BEHELD, MADAME VASSON --
SPARE ME YOUR SIMPERING, BOY.

IT'S WHAT WE AGREED TO THAT MATTERS.
ALL OF US HAVE SUFFERED AT HER HANDS. ALL OF US HAVE LOST.
WE FORMED THIS COALITION TO SEE HER PAY FOR HER CRIMES. CRIMES AGAINST ALL OF US...

...SHE KILLED KURTIS'S PARTNERS...

...SHE MURDERED MADAME VASSON'S HUSBAND...

...SHE SLAUGHTERED TWELVE OF MY MEN.
AND I WOULDN'T THINK IT NECESSARY TO REMIND YOU OF YOUR FIANCÉE...

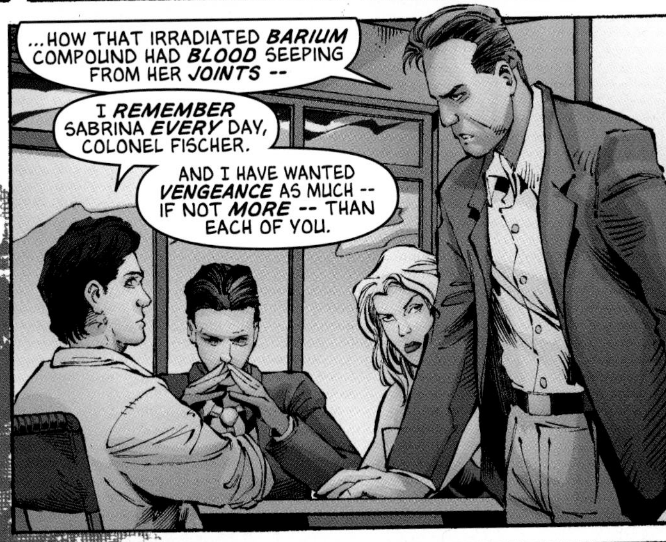

...HOW THAT IRRADIATED BARIUM COMPOUND HAD BLOOD SEEPING FROM HER JOINTS --
I REMEMBER SABRINA EVERY DAY, COLONEL FISCHER.
AND I HAVE WANTED VENGEANCE AS MUCH -- IF NOT MORE -- THAN EACH OF YOU.

BUT WANTING ELEKTRA DEAD AND KILLING HER ARE TWO DIFFERENT THINGS.
AND I TOLD YOU ALL WHEN THIS BEGAN, I WOULD NEVER BE PARTY TO THE LATTER.

ELEKTRA KNOWS WHAT SHE IS, NOW. SHE'S BEEN FORCED TO ADMIT IT.
WITH THAT UNDERSTANDING, SHE CAN COME TO ONLY ONE CONCLUSION...

...DESERVE TO LIVE...
...DESERVE TO DIE...
WHY AM I ALIVE?
SSSSS

WILL YOU DO IT?
WILL YOU DO IT FOR ME?
SSSS
OR DO I HAVE TO DO IT MYSELF?
THANK YOU...
...FOR MAKING IT EASY...

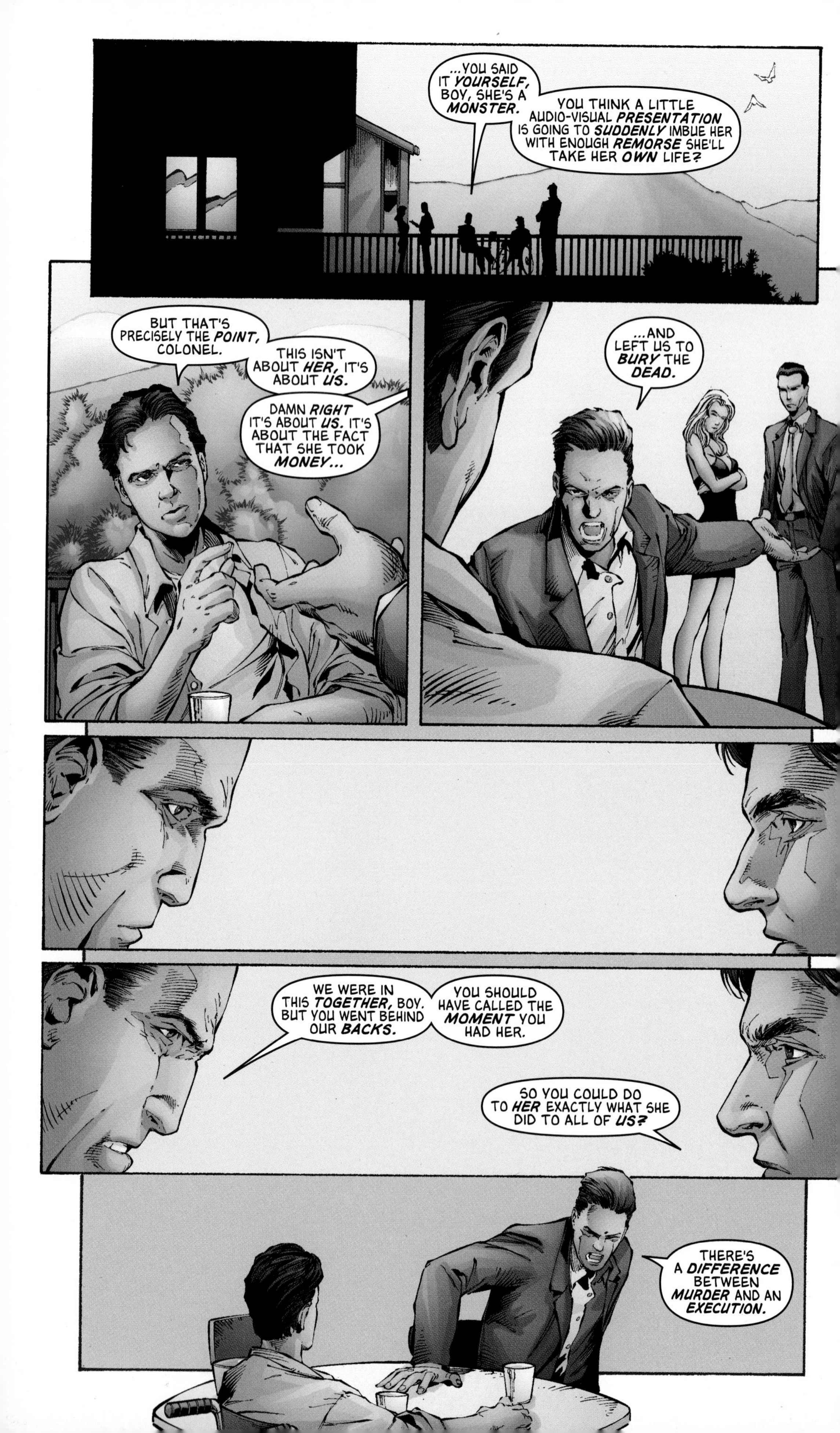
...YOU SAID IT YOURSELF, BOY, SHE'S A MONSTER.
YOU THINK A LITTLE AUDIO-VISUAL PRESENTATION IS GOING TO SUDDENLY IMBUE HER WITH ENOUGH REMORSE SHE'LL TAKE HER OWN LIFE?
BUT THAT'S PRECISELY THE POINT, COLONEL.
THIS ISN'T ABOUT HER, IT'S ABOUT US.
DAMN RIGHT IT'S ABOUT US. IT'S ABOUT THE FACT THAT SHE TOOK MONEY...
...AND LEFT US TO BURY THE DEAD.
WE WERE IN THIS TOGETHER, BOY. BUT YOU WENT BEHIND OUR BACKS.
YOU SHOULD HAVE CALLED THE MOMENT YOU HAD HER.
SO YOU COULD DO TO HER EXACTLY WHAT SHE DID TO ALL OF US?
THERE'S A DIFFERENCE BETWEEN MURDER AND AN EXECUTION.

NOT TO ME.
THEN MORE THAN YOUR LEGS ARE CRIPPLED.
COLONEL --
JUST SHUT UP, LOCKE.
JUST SHUT UP.
WE HAVE SOME THINGS WE NEED TO DISCUSS, JEREMY.
OF COURSE YOU DO.
TAKE HOWEVER LONG YOU LIKE, NOLAN...
...BUT EVEN IF YOU CHANGE THE SPELLING, IT'LL STILL BE CALLED MURDER.

‹...PLEASE, PAPA...›
‹...I TRIED I'M SORRY I DIDN'T MEAN TO...›
‹...PLEASE DON'T PLEASE DON'T HIT...›

‹...PA...›
‹...PAPA...?›
‹...NO PLEASE PAPA I'M **SORRY** PAPA...›
‹...NOT... NOT **AGAIN** PAPA...›

...MONSTER...
...ANOTHER MONSTER...
...SAME MONSTER...

...FINISHED...
"CAN I ASK YOU A QUESTION, MISTER LOCKE?"

GO AHEAD.
IF YOU'RE SO OPPOSED TO KILLING ELEKTRA, WHY DIDN'T WE JUST HAND HER OVER TO THE COPS WHILE SHE WAS HERE?
MOSTLY BECAUSE IT'D BE IMPOSSIBLE TO CONVICT HER.
ALL THE EVIDENCE YOU AND I GATHERED WOULD BE INADMISSIBLE. SO ANY TRIAL WOULD HAVE BEEN A JOKE...
...AND THAT'S ASSUMING SHE GOT TO TRIAL, AND SHE WOULDN'T HAVE.
WE HAD HER HERE FOR TWENTY-FOUR HOURS, DRUGGED THE ENTIRE TIME, AND EVEN WITH THAT SHE NEARLY ESCAPED.
BUT THIS WAY --
WE'LL TALK ABOUT IT LATER. LOOKS LIKE THE COALITION HAS REACHED A DECISION.
YOU HAVE REACHED A DECISION, HAVEN'T YOU?
WE HAVE.
WHATEVER YOUR REASONS, AND FRANKLY, WHATEVER OURS, YOU TOOK A HUGE LIBERTY, BOY.
YOU LET THE MONSTER GO.

EVEN IF WE DIDN'T HAVE A PERSONAL STAKE, THAT'S STILL UNFORGIVABLE.
SO NOW SHE'S OUT THERE. AND SHE WON'T EVER STOP.
I THINK YOU'RE WRONG.
MAYBE. BUT MAYBE DON'T CUT IT.
WE NEED TO BE SURE.
YOUR MAN HERE IS GOING TO TELL US WHERE HE DROPPED ELEKTRA.
I'VE GOT SOME PEOPLE I CAN SCRAMBLE, WE'LL HEAD OUT THERE ASAP, SEE IF WE CAN PICK UP THE TRAIL.
IF YOU'RE RIGHT, WE'LL FIND HER GROWING COLD.
AND IF YOU DON'T, YOU'LL MAKE HER THAT WAY?
THAT'S RIGHT.
AND IF MISTER CARSON REFUSES?
WE'D RATHER HE DIDN'T...
...WE'D RATHER DO IT THE EASY WAY.
I SEE.

I COULD HAVE STOPPED FISCHER.
HE'S NOT AS FAST AS HE THINKS HE IS.
FORGET ABOUT IT.
WHAT IS IT WITH YOU?
THEY'RE GOING TO KILL HER! I THOUGHT YOU DIDN'T WANT THAT!
THIS IS ABOUT CONSCIENCE.
YOU SOUND LIKE THEM, CARSON!
HOW MANY TIMES DO I HAVE TO SAY THIS?

...THIS COLD IN THE MIDDLE OF THE DESERT?
HERE, LET ME --
THEY'VE FOUND THE TRAIL.
THEY'RE LOOKING WITH INFRARED NOW.
SHE COULDN'T HAVE GONE FAR.
IF THEY FIND HER, I WANT TO BE THERE.
I NEED TO SEE HER DIE.
WE'LL ALL BE THERE.
BRAVO ONE, BRAVO ONE, COME IN.
BRAVO ONE, GO.
THINK WE'VE GOT HER...
GIVE ME A GPS LOCATION, WE'LL BE RIGHT THERE...

...AND FOR GOD'S SAKE, DON'T APPROACH HER!
BRAVO ONE, NO WORRY...
...SHE'S DONE.

ISSUE #14
Greg H.

HOLLYWOOD HILLS.

MISTER LOCKE?
PHONE CALL.
IT'S FISCHER.
THANK YOU, PHILLIP.
GO AHEAD, COLONEL.
GOT SOME NEWS FOR YOU, LOCKE.
COUPLE OF MY BOYS RADIOED 'BOUT FIVE MINUTES AGO...

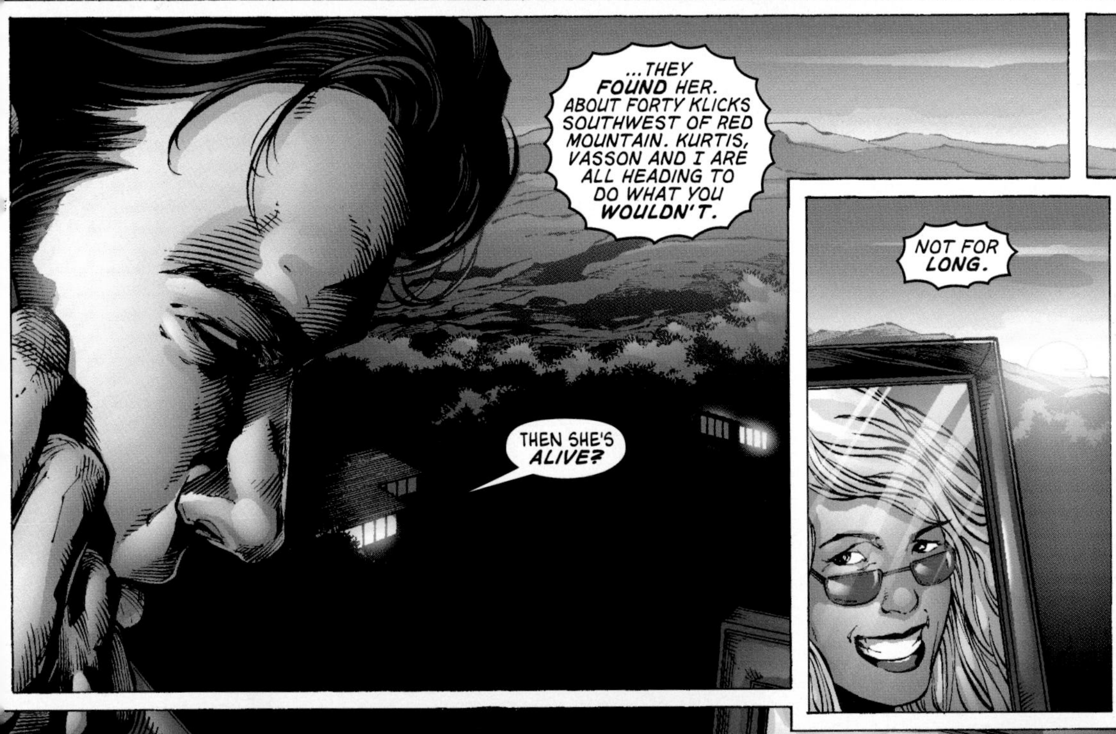
...THEY FOUND HER. ABOUT FORTY KLICKS SOUTHWEST OF RED MOUNTAIN. KURTIS, VASSON AND I ARE ALL HEADING TO DO WHAT YOU WOULDN'T.
THEN SHE'S ALIVE?
NOT FOR LONG.

THE MOJAVE DESERT.
IT'S GONNA BE HOT TODAY.
WHAT IS THAT, IS THAT SOME KIND OF COSTUME?

DUNNO.
SHE'S NOT TOO BAD ON THE EYES, YOU CLEAN HER UP.
CLEAN HER UP A LOT, DUDE.

COLONEL SAYS STAY CLEAR OF HER.
YEAH, WE KNOW...
...JUST SEEMS A WASTE THAT'S ALL.

SHE EVEN BREATHING?
THINK SO.
WANT TO CHECK?
›SKSS‹ BRAVO TWO, BRAVO TWO, SITREP?
BRAVO TWO, WE'RE SECURE, COLONEL. EVERYTHING'S QUIET.
›SKSS‹ AFFIRM. WE ARE APPROXIMATELY FOUR MINUTES FROM YOUR LOCATION, OVER.

UNDERSTOOD. WE'LL BE WAITING. OUT.
YOU KNOW WHAT THIS IS? THIS IS SILK...
...THAT'S WHAT THIS IS. SILK.
THAT LIKE UNDERWEAR?
NAH, LIKE LINGERIE, SEE?

DON'T THINK SHE'S WEARING ANYTHING UNDER --
--GAHH!
WHAT? WHAT?
SHE MOVED SHE MOVED --
SHE'S ALIVE, DUDE! SHE'S STILL ALIVE!
DAMMIT, I TOLD YOU TWO TO LEAVE HER ALONE!
ALL RIGHT.
YOU GUYS COVER ME, I'M GONNA BIND HER, JUST TO BE SURE.

SHE MOVED, I SWEAR TO GOD SHE HIT ME --
WOULD YOU SHUT UP, TONKINS?
DAMN DEAD WEIGHT...
...WON'T STAY STILL...
SHE'S FAKING IT, SHE'S FAKING --
TONKINS! I TOLD YOU --
-- SHUT THE HELL UP!

INTROSPECT PART FOUR
BUT...BUT THEY HAD HER THEY SAID... THEY SAID...
YOU SAID THEY WERE GOOD, COLONEL! YOU SAID THEY KNEW HOW TO HANDLE HER!
HOW COULD SHE... THERE WERE FOUR OF THEM!
BLAME LOCKE.
THE DAMN FOOL'S PLAN BACK-FIRED...

...SHE'S NOT LOOKING TO KILL HERSELF.
SHE'S JUST LOOKING TO KILL.
SHE KILLED ALL OF THEM. FOUR SOLDIERS, SHE JUST --
OF COURSE SHE DID, MADAME VASSON!
IT'S WHAT SHE DOES. SHE'S A PREDATOR --
THIS ONE'S MISSING HIS GEAR.
SHE TOOK HIS THINGS, COLONEL.
THE GUN, THE GRENADES, THE AMMUNITION, THE WATER --
>SKSSS< AND THE RADIO.

›SKSS‹ --THREE, READ YOU, COLONEL.
GET THE BIRD IN HERE, NOW! TRANSPONDER LOCK ON MY POSITION, WE ARE TAKING FIRE --
-- REPEAT WE ARE TAKING FIRE! HOSTILE IS ARMED, BRAVO TWO NEGATIVE FUNCTION!
UNDERSTOOD AND EN ROUTE. E.T.A. THREE MINUTES. WILL ADVISE --
NEGATIVE, NEGATIVE! HOSTILE HAS COMS ACCESS, REPEAT COMS ACCESS. GO DARK...
...I SAY AGAIN, GO DARK.
BRAVO THREE, RECEIVE AND UNDERSTOO
GOIN DAR

NGHGG
HHGUHHUHUH
BRAVO THREE! BRAVO THREE, DAMMIT, COME IN!
WHAT IS THAT, WHAT DOES THAT MEAN?
SHE'S GOT A RADIO, VALERIY. SHE CAN HEAR EVERYTHING WE BROADCAST.
WE WON'T BE MAKING ANY MORE CALLS UNTIL THEY ARRIVE.
THEY SAID IT WOULD TAKE THREE MINUTES?
THAT'S RIGHT.
WE'LL... WE'LL BE ALL RIGHT, YES? FOR THREE MINUTES?
SURE.
HNNHU... HU-HELP...

...KUKU-
COLONEL
HELP...
...CAN-CAN'T
WALK SHE SHOT
M-MY LEG...
...PLEASE
HELP...
...SHE'LL
KILL ME I CAN'T
WA-WALK...
CAN'T DO
IT, KURTIS...
...SHE MADE YOU BAIT. WE
TRY FOR YOU, AND SHE'LL
CUT US APART.
BRAVO THREE'LL BE
HERE IN TWO MINUTES.
YOU GOT TO HOLD ON,
OR GET OUT OF THERE
YOURSELF.
NHUH
HUHUH

NHAA!
PHUP
PHUP
STOP!
...PLEASE STOP...
WHY IS SHE DOING THIS?
I'M BEGGING YOU PLEASE...
BECAUSE SHE KNOWS WE CAN'T STOP HER.
SHE'S AN ANIMAL, PURE AND SIMPLE.
SHE'S A BEAST --
-- A DISGUSTING BEAST!

YOU'RE A THING, YOU UNDERSTAND ME? YOU'RE NOT HUMAN, YOU'RE A PREDATOR, SOME SORT OF MONSTER!
HE'S NOT THREATENING YOU!
LEAVE HIM ALONE!
DAMMIT! I KNOW YOU HEAR ME, ELEKTRA!
ANSWER ME!
THERE! THERE!

SITREP, SIR?
SHE'S PUT DOWN ABOUT A CLIP AND A HALF. SHE'S GOT FLYNN'S PACK, GEAR AND HIS WATER.
SHE CAN'T RUN FAR --
SHE'S NOT RUNNING!
SHE'S HUNTING --
WHAT IS THE PILOT DOING...?

SHE... SHE COULDN'T...?
MOVE! MOVE!!

MINIMAL INJURIES, BUT WE'RE SCREWED ON TRANSPORT, SIR.
THE HELL WITH THE RANSPORT!
NONE OF US RE GETTING OUT OF RE AS LONG AS SHE'S OUT THERE, DON'T YOU GET THAT?
I WANT A FULL SWEEP, AND YOU TELL THE MEN, THEY SO MUCH AS THINK THEY SEE HER, THEY OPEN FIRE.
AND ONCE SHE'S DOWN...
...SHOOT HER AGAIN.
I DON'T WANT DENTALS FOR RECOGNITION, UNDERSTOOD? I DON'T WANT ANY PART OF HER LEFT.
SIR, YES SIR.
NOLAN? NOLAN, IT'S ALL RIGHT, YOU'RE GOING TO BE FINE...
VALERIY, I DON'T LIKE CALLING YOU A LIAR...
...BUT WE ARE ABOUT AS FAR FROM FINE AS YOU CAN GET.
RIGHT, SQUAD, LISTEN UP! COLONEL WANTS A SWEEP, YOU SEE THE HOSTILE, YOU SHOOT TO KILL...

WHAT THE --?
GET OVER THERE!
AND FOR GOD SAKE, ST SHARP
DALTON? DALTON?
MORGAN, CLOSE UP, RIGHT NOW --

-- SHE'S PICKING US OFF...
...ONE BY ONE...
WHAT THE HELL IS GOING ON HERE?
...NO...

WE WON'T SURVIVE THE NIGHT.

COLONEL... LIAM?
WE WON'T SURVIVE THE NIGHT.
SHE CAN'T HAVE GOTTEN ALL OF THEM.

THAT'D BE TEN MEN, TEN TRAINED --
OH MY GOD.

THE ROAD IS DUE SOUTH...
...THE WATER IN THE CANTEEN WILL LAST UNTIL YOU REACH IT...
...IF YOU'RE LUCKY.

ISSUE #15
Greg Horn

ERROR - ALL ZONES
F1
F2
F3
ENTER
LOCKE.
LOCKE.

ELEKT--
NO, SHH...
...HUSH NOW, MISTER JEREMY LOCKE.
YOU DON'T TALK, YOU LISTEN.
YOUR SOLDIERS ARE ALL DEAD, LOCKE.
THEY CAME TO KILL ME AND I SLAUGHTERED THEM ALL.

NTROSPECT PART FIVE

SCARED?
HELL YES.
HMM...
...THAT'S GOOD.
IT'S WHAT YOU'D EXPECT, ISN'T IT?
AND YOU WERE RIGHT.

I AM A MONSTER.
I WILL DO WHAT A MONSTER DOES.
I WILL KILL YOU.
I DIDN'T LIE --
I SAID HUSH --
-- NO, ELEKTRA, LISTEN --
-- I NEVER LIED --
--GHUUH

I SAID HUSH.
WHY?
YOU'VE KILLED CARSON --
-- YOU'RE GOING TO KILL ME --
-- WHY IN EIGHT HELLS DOES IT MATTER IF I'M SILENT OR NOT?

BECAUSE IT'S WHAT I WANT.
ELEKTRA! IT WASN'T MUHH --
-- HNN WASN'T ME WASN'T CARSON IT WAS THE --
-- OTHERUHNK-UKK --
--KNNGGG

YOU WILL GIVE ME *ONE* THING BEFORE I TAKE YOUR *LIFE* --
-- ONE *ANSWER* --
-- NO *LIES*
WHY HAVE YOU *DONE* THESE THINGS TO *ME,* JEREMY LOCKE?
WHY?

WHY L THESE AMES?
THERE WAS NO GAME!
DAMMIT, I WAS TRYING TO HELP YOU --
-- UHKK
HELP?
DESTROYING ME.
THAT IS YOUR HELP?
DRUGGING ME?
HUNTING ME?
SHAMING ME?
THAT WAS YOUR HELP?
...NO... OTHER... WAY...

ALL I EVER *KAFF* WANTED WAS FOR YOU TO SEE WHAT YOU TRULY ARE.
I JUST... I DIDN'T KNOW ANOTHER WAY.
I HAD TO FORCE YOU TO LOOK.
BUT I'VE NEVER WANTED YOU DEAD.
YOU SENT SOLDIERS --
NO, IT WASN'T ME.
THEY WERE MERCENARIES, WORKING FOR COLONEL FISCHER.
FISCHER, VASSON, KURTIS -- WE WERE A COALITION.

I DON'T KNOW THOSE NAMES.
I'M TELLING YOU THE TRUTH.
ALL I'VE EVER WANTED WAS FOR YOU TO SEE WHAT YOU TRULY ARE.
THEY'RE LIKE ME. PEOPLE YOU HURT.
BUT UNLIKE ME, THEY WANTED YOUR BLOOD.
THEY WANTED YOU DEAD.
I WAS GOING TO DO IT.

IN THE DESERT.
I THOUGHT YOU MIGHT BE RIGHT.
EVERYTHING YOU SAID.
EVERYTHING YOU SHOWED ME.
WHAT YOU SAY I AM.
A MONSTER.

I WAS WILLING TO DIE.
I STILL AM.
I'M TIRED.
I'M TIRED, AND I REALLY DON'T KNOW WHAT YOUR FRIEND IS WAITING FOR...
...HE SHOULD HAVE SHOT ME BY NOW.
WHAT?

PHILLIP, STOP.
JUST PUT THE GUN *DOWN.*
NO, PHILLIP. DON'T.

AND DON'T *WASTE* TIME --

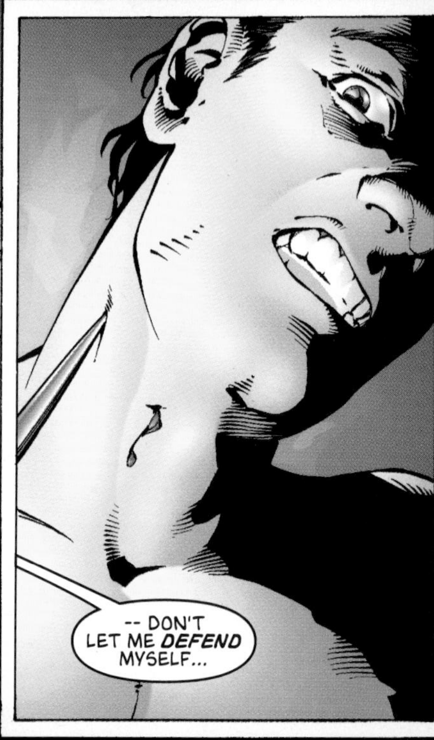
-- DON'T LET ME *DEFEND* MYSELF...

...OR I'LL KILL YOU, TOO.
ISN'T THIS WHAT YOU WANTED? SUICIDE BY ANOTHER NAME?
YOU SAID I DID NOT DESERVE TO LIVE!
YOU SAID IT!
DON'T DO IT
I DID.
BUT THAT DOESN'T MEAN I WANT YOU DEAD.
WHAT ELSE IS THERE?

WHAT ARE YOU WAITING FOR? DAMN YOU --
-- DO IT OR I DO HIM!
PHILLIP, LISTEN TO ME...
...DON'T GIVE THIS TO HER...
...DON'T MAKE IT THIS EASY...
...DON'T LET IT BE SIMPLE.
KILL ME DAMN YOU DO IT --
-- PLEASE JUST DO IT...

YOU WANT TO *DIE,* DO IT *YOURSELF.*
UNLESS YOU WANT TO *LIVE.*

DAMN YOU!
DAM YOU BOT
WHAT IS IT?
WHAT DO YOU WANT FROM ME?
I'VE ALREADY TOLD YOU.
I WANT YOU TO CHANGE.

ELEKTRA.
AND YOU'VE BEEN A MURDERER IN BOTH.

TIME TO BE SOMETHING ELSE.

TWO LIVES.
MAYBE THERE IS NOTHING ELSE I CAN BE.
DO YOU REALLY BELIEVE THAT?
SOME PEOPLE NEED TO DIE.

THAT'S NOT AN ANSWER.
EVEN IF IT WAS, IT'S GROSSLY SIMPLISTIC.

IT'S NOT GOING TO BE SIMPLE ANYMORE, ELEKTRA.

WE'LL DISCUSS THIS LATER.
I DON'T THINK YOU'RE IN ANY CONDITION TO TALK ABOUT IT NOW.
YOU NEED A SHOWER AND A MEAL, AND CERTAINLY A GOOD NIGHT'S SLEEP.
HUFF
GOOD THROW.
HERE.
DOESN'T GO WITH MY DECOR.
PHILLIP WILL SHOW YOU TO THE GUEST ROOM.
SEE YOU IN THE MORNING.

COME ON.

HERE YOU GO.
JEREMY'S MY EMPLOYER AND MY FRIEND.
BUT HE'S AN IDEALIST.
THAT'S NOT SOMETHING I SUFFER FROM.
SEE, I DON'T THINK YOU CAN CHANGE, EVE IF YOU WANT TO.
MAYBE YOU'RE NOT A MONSTER, BUT YOU'RE SURE AS HELL AN ANIMAL.
A DANGEROUS AND VIOLENT ANIMAL.
I'LL BE WATCHING YOU.
AND MAYBE THE TIME'LL COME YOU'LL KILL US BOTH.
BUT I'LL SURE AS HELL TRY TO TAKE YOU WITH US.
YOU HAVE A GOOD NIGHT.
END

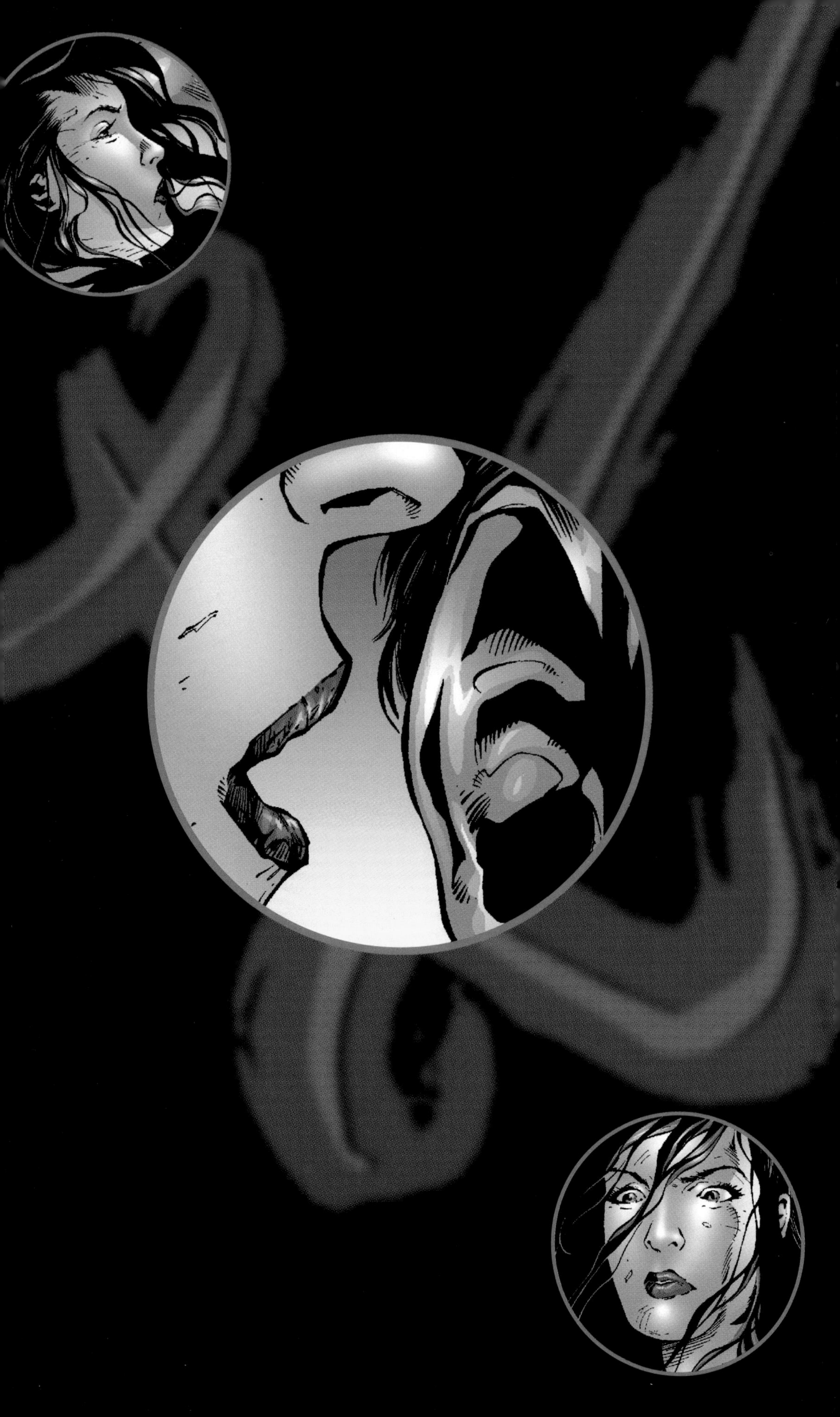

MARVEL KNIGHTS:
DOUBLE-SHOT #3
GLEN FABR -01

STAN LEE PRESENTS:
ELEKTRA: TRUST
GREG RUCKA writer GREG HORN artist
RS/COMICRAFT/JB letters STUART MOORE editor
KELLY LAMY associate managing editor
NANCI DAKESIAN managing editor
JOE QUESADA chief BILL JEMAS president
BUS STOP
local
7am 4pm
10am 7pm
COFFEE
21 BERKELEY
Dicken's

SOFA KING
"Our prices are Sofa King Low!"
BL-BLI-Blip!
YES?
GOLDEN GATE PARK, THE TEA GARDEN. FORTY MINUTES.
BENCH OUTSIDE. PUT THE BAG BENEATH THE BENCH...
...THEN WALK AWAY.
BUT WAIT --
BAY COFFEE
AXI

APEX STUDIOS
...CAN'T JUST PULL THE PLUG ON THE PROJECT --
IT'S ALMOST EIGHTY MILLION OVER BUDGET, GABE!
YOU'VE SEEN THE DAILIES --
YEAH, AND THEY'RE CRAP.
DYLAN ROLLINS IS AN ACADEMY AWARD WINNING DIRECTOR AND PRIMA DONNA.
HE'S GOT A CONTRACT THAT GIVES HIM COMPLETE CONTROL OVER HIS FILMS.
WE'RE NOT EVEN SUPPOSED TO TALK TO HIM.
HE'S AN EGOMANIAC AND HE'S OUT OF CONTROL AND HIS MOVIE'S GONNA DO NOTHING BUT LOSE MONEY.
IT'S JUST MY CAREER WE'RE TALKING ABOUT... CHRISSY!
YOU'RE THE ONE WHO GAVE IT THE GREEN LIGHT, ANN.
DON'T REMIND ME.

YES, ANN?
WHAT THE HELL IS THIS ONE, THIS ONE ABOUT MY LAPTOP?
SOME WOMAN CALLED SHE SAID SHE FOUND IT THAT'S ALL...
FOUND IT? I THOUGHT IT WAS STOLEN WHEN YOU WERE IN SAN FRANCISCO.
SO DID I.

I'VE GOT TO GET BACK TO WORK.
SURE. LOOK, ANN, DON'T WORRY ABOUT IT...
...IT'LL ALL WORK OUT.

E-H
NO TRESSPASSING
YOU FOUND THE **FILE** --
AND I TRANSFERRED THE MONEY. I'LL MOVE THE REST ON **COMPLETION.**
OF COURSE. **WHEN** --
WHEN I'M READY, NO SOONER.
THERE IS SOME **URGENCY** --
CLOSED SET FILMING IN PROGRESS
WHEN I'M READY, NO SOONER, MS. PEERY.
...
...YOU KNOW WHO I AM.
YES.
I SUPPOSE THAT MEANS I HAVE TO **TRUST** YOU.
I SUPPOSE THAT MEANS I HAVE NO **CHOICE.**
SECURITY
THERE ARE **ALWAYS** CHOICES, MS. PEERY.
YOU CAN **CALL** THIS **OFF** RIGHT **NOW.**
I ... I CAN'T...
KWAN

MS. PEERY, UNDERSTAND SOMETHING.
WE'VE MADE A **CONTRACT.**
YOU'VE AGREED TO PAY ME.
I'VE AGREED TO **SOLVE** YOUR PROBLEM.
EACH OF US **TRUSTS** THE OTHER TO NOT DO ANYTHING **STUPID.**
UNDERSTAND?
ROLLINS
...YES...
...YES, I UNDERSTAND.
ROLLIN

WAREHOUSES
E-H
NO TRESSPASSING
Guro's Catering
...HELL PROBLEM WITH THE LIGHTS?
CLOSED SET FILMING IN PROGRESS
YOU PEOPLE HAD ALL NIGHT TO SET THIS UP!
I CAN'T BELIEVE THIS! AM I ALONE HERE?
ON IT, MISTER ROLLINS, RIGHT ON IT --

ROLLINS
KILL ALL OF YOU, I SWEAR I WILL.
WHERE THE HELL IS MY TEA? MY CHAI TEA?
I'LL GO GET IT.

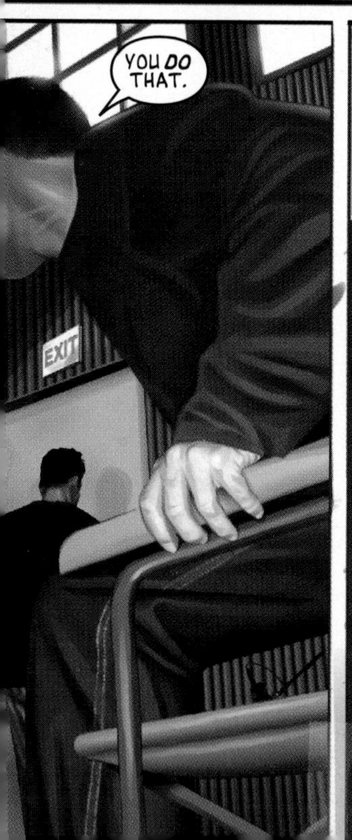
YOU DO THAT.
EXIT

BROWN-NOSE --

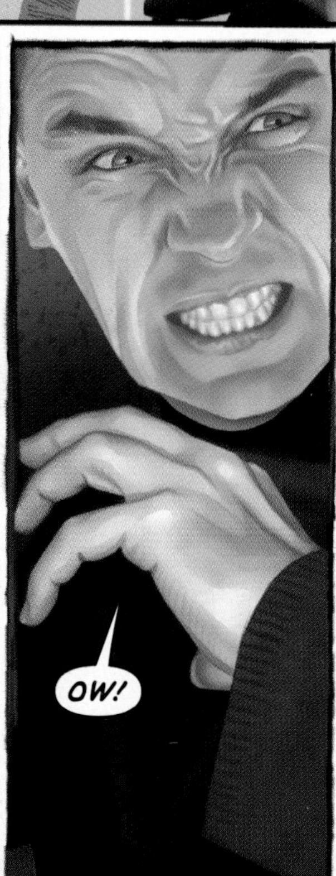
OW!

SOMETHING JUST BIT ME!

CHAI TEA, SOY MOO, VANILLA.
THAT FOR HIS LORD GOD?
Gyro's Catering
DON'T LET HIM HEAR YOU SAY THAT.
SORRY, BAD JOKE.
NAH, IT'S WHAT I WANT TO CALL HIM, *TOO.*
THANKS!
Gyro's Catering
AMBULANCE
AMBULANCE

APEX STUDIOS
...ANSWER TO YOUR *PRAYERS.*
GABE! THE MAN'S *DEAD!*
SORRY, BAD TASTE.
YOU FOUND A NEW DIRECTOR YET?
I'VE MADE A FEW CALLS.
I HEARD SCOTT'S INTERESTED.
AMONGST OTHERS. WE'LL BE FINE.
LOOKS LIKE -- HEY!
YOU GOT YOUR *LAPTOP* BACK!
YEAH. THE PERSON WHO FOUND IT SENT IT BACK THIS MORNING.
VERY COOL.
GUESS THERE ARE STIL *SOME* PEOPLE O THERE WORTH OF *TRUST,* HUH?
HOLLY
YEAH. GUESS SO.
the end

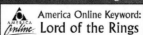

SUBSCRIBERS... ASSEMBLE
SUBSCRIBE AND SAVE!
1 Title For $23.97- A savings of $3!
2 Titles For $22.97- A savings of $8!
3 Or More Titles For $21.97 each- A savings of $15 or more!
MARVEL HEROES
❑ AVE Avengers
❑ BPR Black Panther
❑ CAM Captain America
❑ CMV Captain Marvel
❑ FAN Fantastic Four
❑ INC Hulk
❑ IRM Iron Man
❑ THO Thor
❑ BLT Thunderbolts
❑ CAL The Call Of Duty NEW!
MARVEL ULTIMATES
❑ ULA The Ultimates
❑ USP Ultimate Spider-Man
❑ UXM Ultimate X-Men
X-MEN
❑ CAB Soldier X (Cable)
❑ DDP Agent X (Deadpool)
❑ EXL Exiles
❑ XME Uncanny X-Men
❑ WOL Wolverine
❑ XFO X-Statix (X-Force)
❑ MEN New X-Men
❑ XTR X-Treme X-Men
MARVEL KNIGHTS
❑ DDV Daredevil
❑ ELK Elektra (Mature Readers)
❑ PUN Punisher (Mature Readers)
SPIDER-MAN
❑ AMZ Amazing Spider-Man
❑ SPI Peter Parker, Spider-Man
❑ TAW Spider-Man: Tangled Web
❑ SPG Spider-Girl
LIMITED TIME HEROES OFFER
❑ Yes! I want both Avengers and Incredible Hulk for just $37.94
A Savings of $16.00!
Exclusive Subscriber Savings and Services
Your satisfaction guaranteed or your money back on all remaining issues!
IMPROVED PACKAGING!
All issues are mailed with cardboard backing in new weather resistant cellophane bags!
Ordering is fast and easy!
❑ Yes! Sign me up for home delivery of the comics I've checked. I deserve the most in savings, convenience, service, and selection!
My satisfaction is guaranteed!
Check off the subscriptions you want delivered to your home (12 issues each) and return this page or a copy to:
MARVEL ENTERTAINMENT GROUP, INC.
P.O. BOX 32 NEWBURGH, NY 12551.
Please provide credit card information or make your check or money order payable to "Marvel Entertainment Group, Inc."
Or order Toll Free at 800-217-9158.
OFFER GOOD UNTIL 12/31/2002.
YES, YOU CAN PHOTOCOPY THIS AD!
Please print:
NAME OF READER
DATE OF BIRTH (M/D/Y)
STREET ADDRESS
E-MAIL
CITY
STATE
ZIP
# of subscriptions
Amount enclosed: $
Charge my: ☐ VISA ☐ MasterCard
CREDIT CARD #
EXPIRATION DATE
NAME OF CREDIT CARD HOLDER (IF DIFFERENT FROM NAME ABOVE)
SIGNATURE FOR CREDIT CARD ORDERS
Canada, add $10.00 per title (in U.S. funds only, includes GST#R127032852). Foreign, add $12 per title in U.S. funds only. Allow 6 to 10 weeks for delivery of your first issue. TM & © 2002 Marvel Enterprises Inc. All rights reserved.
H26MD
WWW.MARVEL.COM
For a comic store near you call 1-800-comicbook
MARVEL